ABOUT THIS BOOK...

We first heard MariJo Moore's stories and poems around the campfire. Very much in the American Indian oral tradition, they should be read aloud. They will touch your heart...

KITUWAH: *The American Indian National Exposition of Arts and Education*

MariJo Moore's *Returning to the Homeland* might be described as an experience of reconciling two worlds, the heritage of two cultures. Her care for the Cherokee beliefs and way of life she discovers is deeply felt and often expressed in fresh and moving images.

Wilma Dykeman
Author of *French Broad* and *Tennessee Woman*

In Returning to the Homeland, the voice of MariJo Moore emerges out of the essence of spirit. It is a voice that reminds us we are the sum total of our past.

Gabriel Horn (White Deer of Autumn)
Author of *Native Heart* and *Ceremony—In the Circle of Life*

MariJo Moore is on a remarkable spiritual journey—back to her people and their ancestral home here in the mountains of North Carolina. We are fortunate, indeed, that through this lovely and evocative book of poems and short stories she shares with us her quest for her Cherokee past.

Marshall DeBruhl
Author of *San Jacinto: A Life of Sam Houston*

In this beautiful collection of poems and short stories, MariJo Moore shares her Cherokee heritage and through her gift for imagery invites the reader to touch the spirit of the mountians and the Cherokee people.

Joan Greene
Archivist, Museum of the Cherokee Indian
Cherokee, North Carolina

The author next to an ancient mountain waterfall of her people.

RETURNING TO THE HOMELAND

Cherokee Poetry and Short Stories

MariJo Moore

WORLDCOMM®
a division of Creativity, Inc.

Alexander, North Carolina

Publisher: Ralph Roberts

Vice-President/Publishing: Pat Roberts

Illustrations: Ellenburg

Interior Design and Typesetting: **WorldComm**®

Cover Art: Ellenburg

Printed in the United States of America
10 9 8 7 6

ISBN 1-56664-073-3

Library of Congress Number: 94-061320

WorldComm—a Division of Creativity, Inc., 65 Macedonia Road, Alexander, North Carolina 28701, (704)252-9515—is a full service publisher.

DEDICATION

For my family, from whom I get my strength,
Tim, with whom I share my love,
and my son, Lance, for whom I continue to write.

ACKNOWLEDGMENTS

I offer the deepest of heartfelt thanks to the following:

Spirit—May you call to many more Eastern Cherokee writers and artists, and offer them open doors.

My Cherokee ancestors—May you always sing in my heart and live in my works.

John Ehle—The sharing of your time and wonderful wisdom means more than you could ever know.

Wilma Dykeman, Joan Greene, Marshall De Bruhl and Gabriel Horn—Your encouraging words are priceless gifts.

Ralph Roberts, Kathryn Hall and Betsy Murphy at WorldComm Publishing—It takes dedicated, hard-working people like you to help awaken olden dreams.

Ellenburg—Kindred spirit, I thank you for sharing your remarkable artistic gifts. May all your work be blessed and all your lessons be gentle.

Marie Junaluska—Not only are you are a great inspiration, this book would not have been complete without the sharing of your expertise of the Cherokee language.

The People of Kituwah—For opening your hearts and allowing me to step safely in, I thank you.

Kathy Doulgas—Your never-ending spiritual support is truly a blessing.

Betty and Sam Maney—Thanks for inviting me into your home, and for listening and understanding.

Timothy Stephens—Thank you for your continuous belief in and support of my calling to these glorious mountains. And thank you for being here when I arrived.

AUTHOR'S NOTE

For many months I had been dreaming of the home-land of my Cherokee ancestors. I knew I was to go to these mountains, to discover the many secrets of old resting in the age-old stones and floating on swift, running waters. To witness the many unburned fires lying in ancient trees.

Perhaps the mountains were dreaming me, calling me to return, for I could get no rest in my soul until I agreed to follow my spirit and move to North Carolina, the place of birth of my family. The land the Creator had given to them so long ago. The land they had struggled to keep but had been forced to leave, walking a trail not of their choosing.

When I first stepped into these mountains, my loneliness became solitude and my prayers turned to gratitude. Tears that had been hiding in my blood for hundreds of years spilled onto my face, unclouding my vision. I had returned home.

It was now time to open my heart to the spirit of my people, to the spirits of place, of the feathered ones and the four-footed ones. To pay attention to the powerful blood that runs in my veins.

The poetry and stories in this book have manifested due to my answering this calling. I ask you to share them with me and to know that one who answers an ancestral calling will never be disappointed.

MariJo Moore
Asheville, North Carolina

CONTENTS

FOREWORD

by John Ehle
Author of *Trail of Tears: The Rise and Fall of the Cherokee Nation*

MariJo Moore has the good fortune of having a Cherokee grandparent on each side of her family, so she has a special call to delve into the labyrinth of Cherokee history and lore, seeking meaning. Here with a poet's charm she commemorates what she has found, and therefore who she is.

As you might know, the Cherokee was the first tribe to create written form for their language. This was well along in their history, in the 1830's. Their story is, therefore, necessarily enhanced by word-of-mouth, generation-by-generation retelling. The journalist and historian seek to separate fact from fiction; the poet is likely to glory in both, and even to favor enhancements, embellishments.

To find one's own roots, as she has done here, is a rewarding experience; librarians admit much of today's labor is helping Americans do so. I for one have enjoyed tracing my people and have gone all the way to 1710 with the Ihli line (original spelling). They were wool weavers and tailors. Documentation of my father's mother's people, the Marsden family, reaches into the

1500s, even to the Scottish kings, provided you will grant me one recognized illegitimacy.

My mother's brothers looked with suspicion on my interest in their knowledge of her ancestry, and my mother appeared to be ashamed of it. By research and chance I have found a host of English, German, Welsh and Scotch-Irish kin, farmers all, including five who were slain in Indian fighting and one who was a captain in the American Revolution.

All of this gives me a sense of being on their earth with deep roots, indeed, and a certain sense of belonging.

MariJo Moore, with Cherokee ancestry, has a particularly distinguished part of the American story to tell. The Cherokee, close to the nurturing earth and nurtured by extended families, represent countless years on this continent. And she, a poet, is able beautifully to clothe the story, and to endow it with emotion, and there's plenty of emotion in the history of the noble Cherokee. Her book is a beautiful incursion into their heritage, as I read it, and beyond that to life, itself--hers and yours and mine. It nurtures the human spirit and renews it.

"GLORY! GLORY! GLORY!"

Chief Rising Fawn expressing his awe of the autumn colored highlands and misty veiled valleys of his Cherokee homeland. Circa 1837.

POLESTAR

Register your dreams with your ancestors
for you were their dreams.

These ancient ladies (yes, they *were* ladies) as they
danced around ceremonial
fires padding their feet into their Mother for
reassurance of long and bountiful
lives for themselves and their children's children.

They collected, polished, loved, and cherished
rocks, stones, beads, and shells
just as their future sisters and daughters
do today.

And they kissed softly the eyelids of winter warriors...
proud beings with spirits of determination
until pushed into rage by the
instinct of survival.

Where are they now?
These ancient ladies who bred, wept, loved, shared.
Whose dark hands kneaded the maize—turned the
sweat into beautiful, beautiful
jewelry, blankets, and care.

Are their memories resting in
the green cornstalks of the fields,
whispering their secrets of old
to the winds?

Are they on the dark wings of starlings?
Under the hidden bellies of snakes?
In the tangled fur of rabbits?
In the soft tears of dew?

They are resting in the pupils of the poetical ghosts
of deep–drinking, soft, soft,
dark, dark, brown, brown eyes
of the sisters and daughters of the ancient ladies.

EVERYONE NEEDS SOMEONE

My granddaddy was a full-blooded Cherokee Indian
with eyes and hair black as tar
and shiny as a crow's back.
My Irish grandmother said
I looked like him.
I hoped so 'cause I liked him.

I liked the way his voice sounded
like soft running water over smooth pebbles
whenever he would tell me to ignore the poor black
children living down the road whenever they would
laugh, point at us and demand
"Talk some Mexican!"

"Sometimes," he would tell me, touching
my crying eyes with a copper-colored hand,
"it's better not to claim you're Injun
in these parts of Tennessee.
Everyone needs someone to look down on.
Everyone."

But my granddaddy died long before I learned the truths
behind stockade forts made of greed
thousands of tears trailing in the snow
unwanted lands reserved
the ridiculous act of termination
and the never-ending stings of discrimination.

Long before he finished telling me the stories
of how our family had to hide out in the caves
of Western North Carolina.
Long before the Cherokee blood in my veins began to
truly overflow the Irish.

And when he died
his eyes no longer shone, his hair was dirty, matted,
and the smooth stones in his voice were muddied gravel.
My granddaddy died drunk and alone
speaking his language
to the stars.

SHAMANIC DANCE

The poet spoke
and the words meshed with my soul.
My spirit so thrilled

so involved
took flight
then returned bringing

gifts from the special realm
where only poets and thieves
are allowed to visit.

Poets because they are to know
and thieves because they dare to touch
what may not be theirs.

I watched him
as he spoke his words.
They tasted good to him

dancing through his sonorous voice
splattering into psyches,
melting the ambiance of the room.

But taste is not enough to feed one's hungry soul.
I knew he was there for a reason
never daring to ask

what this might be.
I simply trusted the powers that be
to allow the poems to sink

their teeth into
whatever part of me
needed to acknowledge them.

Sitting in outside silence,
this dance engulfing my senses

I realized that what I had been dreaming was true.

There is a place in the mountains
where I can discover who I am.
A place where my spirit will be set free.

And when this poet said
"Remember, the first great law states:
All power comes from women!"

The Cherokee blood in
my veins
flowed with approval.

STARS ARE BIRDS

An old man told his grandson that stars are birds.

"How do you know this, Papa?" the child asked in surprise. The old man looked deeply into his grandson's heart and saw that the blood of his lineage was asleep. He then knew that the time had come.

"You do not know about the stories of your ancestors. It is time you learn. I will tell some of them to you.

"We know that the stars are birds, for one day a Cherokee man saw one fall to earth from the heavens. He searched in the exact place the star had fallen and there he found a tiny bird, no larger than a newly hatched chicken. This is how we know the stars are birds."

The young boy did not want to dispute his grandfather's word but this story was not too convincing. He decided to ask another question. "And the Arm in the Sky, Papa. Are those stars birds, also?"

"Yes. The seven stars that look as a human's arm bent at the elbow are seven birds that fly together. They will not fall because they are as a tribe, always traveling side by side."

His grandson looked doubtful, but the old man continued.

"Do you know the reason of the Milky Way? One story is that there were once two hunters in the sky:

One who lived in the northern part and hunted big game, and one who lived in the southern part and hunted small game.

The northern hunter was brave and came to the southern hunter's land and stole his wife as she was grinding corn. He carried her far away to his home in the North, leaving her tiny dog behind to eat the meal that was spilled. But soon the dog began to follow the pair, the meal spilling from his mouth as he traveled across the sky, making the Milky Way, which the Cherokee call to this day *Gil' LiUtsun'Stanun'yi*, which means 'Where the dog ran'."

This the young boy could relate to since he himself had a small dog that was always hungry. His interest piqued, he asked his grandfather an even more difficult question. "Where did our people come from?" The old man smiled. The olden blood in the veins of his grandson had now begun to stir.

"The first man and woman and the sun and the moon, which are brother and sister, were all created in a time of long ago by beings who came from the upper world. They left the sun and moon in charge. One to rule by day and one to rule by night."

"I see," said the child. Then, as an afterthought he added, "Do you believe all of these stories, Papa?"

"It matters not what I believe, it matters why I believe."

"What do you mean?"

"Those of my people who have walked this earth before me have said these things, and it gives me great comfort to know they cared enough to make sure these beliefs were passed on to me as I am now passing them to you."

At this the young boy looked satisfied, so therefore was the old man satisfied. In silent agreement they looked into each other's eyes, and thus the stories continued.

IN THESE MOUNTAINS

As dreams begin to dance themselves awake
after a day of full flushing rains
in these mountains
the bronze hands of women
reach from beneath the earth
their bones glowing like neon fishes in cave waters.

Droplets pelt the underfur of delicate wild flowers
steam rises to kiss moistened lips of falling leaves
while I wander around inside the past
watching, waiting
hearing the bronze women calling
my name.

Memories unfold from around these
glorious ancestral mountains
positioning themselves into low hanging fog
touching the soft breasts of those who pay attention
as the rains fall down into running waters
stopping only when instructed so by the Thunder Being.

Sweet tobacco smells rise from the white water falling
and I taste the aroma as it floats into my being.
This is when the memories come close enough to smell
but not close enough to touch
just close enough to taste
but never close enough to touch.

And sometimes
late in the afternoon
after it rains all day in these mountains
if I know in just which direction to tilt my head
and if I listen intently
through the raindrops

I can hear gentle, sleepy, rhythmic sounds
of small rounded pebbles
clicking inside tortoise-shell rattles
strapped to the ankles of the bronze women
as they dance the Green Corn Dance
reminding me

I am never alone
in these mountains.

SEEKERS

Close your eyes
float into the distance for a moment
can you see them?

I can see them
walking a trail leading nowhere
camping next to frozen waters

carrying their hearts in thin blankets
wrapped tightly around their pride and dignity.
Some with no blankets at all.

Proud people, they are lost souls
with shattered dreams and broken spirits
wandering, looking for a way back to their homeland.

Mostly Elders, beautiful children, and young mothers,
who became confused and sick, dying and losing
their direction while walking a
trail they did not choose.

Pray for them, pray for these seekers
pray they find the way back to their homeland
so they may rest.

Can you see them?
Walking a trail leading nowhere
camping beside frozen waters.

I can see them
walking, searching,
crying...

SOME SAY

You look Indian some say
and I know what they mean.

Black hair, blacker eyes, and a defiant chin
which stretches forward when I walk.

You don't look Indian some say
and I know what they mean.

No feathers dangling from my hair,
no braids hanging down my back.

You seem Indian some say
and I know what they mean.

Quiet self-determination aided by an
in-depth spiritual knowledge of things and people.

You don't seem Indian some say
and I know what they mean.

No wanting to revenge the past,
no desire to cover the truth.

I knew you were Indian some say
and I know what they mean.

A reverence for the forest, rivers, and mountains,
a profound respect for true wisdom.

I am Cherokee
as was my paternal grandfather
and maternal grandmother.

I hear what some say and yet it doesn't matter.
Not as long as I remain open

to the spirits of those
who have gone before me.

THE COLORED MOUNTAIN

"It's raining colors," Anna says aloud, although there is no one to hear. The early morning rain has given the leaves just the encouragement they need to let go and begin falling, circling invisible foes, and dancing with one another as they make the journey to their chosen resting place. "Yes, it's autumn time again," she smiles, revealing many missing teeth. "Time to go over there behind that colored mountain and rake off that place."

After a meal of sassafras tea and dried apples, she wraps an old yellow knitted shawl about her aging shoulders, adjusts the bright red scarf around her silver hair, and begins to make her way down the path leading from her cabin. She uses a hand-carved hickory walking stick to balance her feeble body as her right leg drags noticeably, leaving strange marks in the dirt. Out of habit, she turns slightly to see if her old shaggy dog Wa'ya is following. It is a full moment before she realizes he has died the winter before. "Of course," she reminds herself, "he will be waiting for me when I get there."

It has been a long while since Anna has been to that place. The last time her granddaughters came to visit, they strictly forbade her to go back there this year. They said it was too long a walk for an old woman, and promised that when the leaves began to fall, they would go and clean it for her. Of course, she knew they wouldn't. They had too many important things to take care of, like making sure their daughters entered the Miss Fall Festival Contest, and making sure their husbands had been spending their time where they said they had. "Oh well, they will soon learn," she chuckles to the crows flying overhead.

A strong wind, gusting from the ridge behind her, almost knocks her to the ground. Her old tattered shawl falls from around her shoulders down to her thick waist, but she doesn't notice. She has something of much importance on her mind. After walking for almost twenty minutes on the rocky path through the forest, she stops by a swollen creek to rest for a spell. Taking the small cloth bag which she keeps pinned underneath her dress, she pulls open the tie strings and takes two pinches of tobacco. One she tosses to the swift, talking waters, and one she slips inside her cheek. Such good sweet, Indian tobacco, grown in her own backyard, refreshes her soul as well as her mouth.

As Anna looks into the waters, she begins to think of her husband. He has been gone to spirit for over ten years now, and still she misses him. As she again begins to walk, she allows thoughts to fill her mind to take the pain away from her tired legs as she climbs the steep mountain path. But the bad memories try to overtake her. The memories of the alcohol and what it did to her husband. How it could turn him from a sweet and gentle man into a raging fool, striking at her and the children.

No one could understand why Anna just didn't leave him—go back to her mama's place in Big Cove and leave him be with his drunken friends. But she couldn't leave him, she loved him. She loved the way he always looked so handsome when his hair was freshly braided. She loved the shine that came to his dark eyes all the six times she had told him she was pregnant. No, she couldn't leave him, so she always forgave him. She knew it wasn't him that did those bad things; it was the alcohol.

"I'm coming, Old Man," she spoke softly under her breath, knowing he could hear her. She supposed he heard everything he wanted to now and was able to know all the time what was going on with the family he had left behind.

Did he remember, as she did now, the times the great grandchildren would come to visit and sit in their laps and ask for stories to be told? Did he know that they never visited now that they were teenagers and had so many more important things to do other than visit their old granny?

Did he think about the two children they had lost: the eldest son and the middle daughter? After the car wreck that took both their lives, he had stopped drinking. He didn't touch a drink for the last twelve years of his life, once he found out that his son was just doing what he had seen his papa do—gotten drunk to forget his troubles.

Anna had been in the back yard working on her herb garden, when they had come to tell her that two of her children had been killed down on Hwy 19, just a few miles west of Bryson City. Why had they even left the reservation?

She had wondered this so many times. Why had they gone out and gotten so drunk and then tried to drive back home early that morning? She would never understand the actions of those who drank so heavily, but she had learned to forgive.

The sun was shining through the leaves in the forest now, forming a splotched pattern on the shawl dragging behind her in the dirt. Anna stopped suddenly as the place came into view. There it was, in the grove of hemlock trees just as she had remembered. She put her walking stick down beside her and begin to clear the dead leaves from the tops of the graves. Only two had distinct markers—large rocks with the names of her children carved on them. She had never allowed anyone to mark the grave of her husband. "I'll always know where I put him," she would tell them. "I don't need a marker to show me."

As she pulled the last of the leaves from the flat ground, she noticed a tiny rock next to the grave of her husband. "Oh, Wa'ya, I almost forgot you. Course, I knew you would be here to greet me."

She lay down in a little clearing not far from the place, spreading her shawl beneath her aching body. "Time for the old woman to take a nap." As her body began to breathe the deep breaths of sleep, she began to dream. And she dreamed the colored mountain was covered with red and green apples; bright, bright oranges; yellow, ripe bananas; and soft, purple grapes. It was as though the Creator had taken huge wagon loads of newly ripened fruit and emptied them down into the lush green valleys for all creatures to enjoy. And walking down the colored mountain was her husband carrying a basket of fresh beautiful fruit.

"It's really good to see you, Anna," he said as he handed her the basket. She saw that he also had a handful of wild flowers picked especially for her. Smiling at him, she turned and looked behind her, but there was nothing there. Taking one last deep breath, her body relaxed. Anna knew she was going to sleep for a long, long time.

VOICES OF THE CHILDREN

A quietness speaks to itself.

Listen, much needed healing is coming
and the little ones are here to participate.
In their souls they know. In their minds they laugh.
The Indian Woman sings to them
Hay-ya, Ha-ya...

The children connect with her
and their voices become as the wind.
Their reverent little arms raise up to the Great Spirit.
To the North, to the East, to the West, to the South
they sing Hay-ya, Ha-ya...

The Spirits dance in the hearts of these children,
patting their seeds into fertile grounds.
Knowing within these moments
within the slivers of moon beams
within the eyes of the hawks

in this surrender of unison
these little ones become
the next Grandfathers and Grandmothers.
As the turtle rattles shake
and the earth begins to dream.

IN THE CAVE

Purple smoke circles around
the old woman as she stirs
the steaming water with a
thin hickory stick.

Taking dried mountain flowers, nuts,
and roots from her bosom
she drops them into the mixture.
This is their only food.

Leaning against the wet, frozen walls
while icy winds howl outside their thoughts,
the Cherokee consider their plight
as they hide from the white soldiers.

There is no distinct smell other than the one of fear
blending with the realization of defeat,
the mixed emotions of survival,
and the moanings of the hungry children.

Some are dying
and yet not weeping.
Some are weeping
and yet not dying.

There are so few left now.
The others have been herded to the West:
the Darkening Land.
Where the sun goes when it dies.

A young girl leans into the belly of her soul
and pleads with the smoky Spirits
to come and take her to their world
so that there might be one less mouth to feed.

The Spirits hear her callings
and abide by her wishes.
They know she just wants relief
from this starvation and deprivation
in the cave.

DAUGHTER OF THE SUN

I entered the din of her silence; she motioned me to sit. Never taking her eyes from her weaving, the Beloved Woman began a story.

the sun did not like the people
such ugly faces were made when they looked at her
but the moon loved the people
so the jealous sun planned to kill them
and sent scorching rays
the Little Men turned one of the people
into a rattlesnake to bite and kill the old sun
but the rattlesnake bit the sun's daughter instead

I have always wanted to have skin as red as yours I said to her, unashamedly. She continued her work and story.

and when the sun found her daughter dead she went
into hiding and grieving and
all the land was darkened
the Little Men instructed the people to go to *Tsvsgina'i*
and when they found the daughter of the sun
dancing with the other ghosts
they struck her head seven times with a stick and put
her into a box and began
to carry her
the long way back to their homes in the east

*I watched as her long hair fell around her shoulders, blend-
ing in with the midnight, moving to Indian time.*

on the long journey she began to plead with them
to please let her out but they refused
the Little Men had told them
not to open the box under any circumstances
but she begged them and begged them
saying she was really dying
so they opened the lid of the box
and out flew a redbird to settle in nearby bushes

*I have waited a long time, I told her. There is but one true
path and I want to know the way.*

when they returned to their homes
and opened the box it was empty
the sun cried and cried for her daughter
until the people danced and sang
causing her to smile and shine though her grief
because the people let the daughter of the sun
fly out of the box we cannot bring back the ghosts
of our people from *Tsvsgina'i*

*Laying down her work, she motioned for me to follow. She
showed me how to touch the future with fingers of intuition
and glimpse the past with guided dreaming. But I could not
capture the total essence of what the Beloved Woman had
said until I began to walk under the waterfalls inside my
own being. Then I began to weave.*

OCONALUFTEE

Intently the river flows
annunciating the healing words
by pounding his fists onto rocks.

Long Man speaks.
I listen.

"The *Ada'ya*—The Mighty Oaks—
have something
to share with you."

I wedge my body
between two naked wooden lovers and
continue to open my heart.

They speak.
I listen.

"Memories are stored in the leaves for a while
then change colors revealing their inner selves
to all who care to be entertained.

Next they go into a period of death
molding into the earth mother
their experiences past.

It is then emptied limbs are
clasped toward father sky,
awaiting a renewal of storings."

They speak.
I listen and I understand.

Life is not a progressive development of mistakes.
Rather it is a cyclical experience
of nature.

To move forward is to share the memories that hurt;
to speak them aloud
is to take the power from them.

To hand the hurt
to *Yihowa*—
The Elder Fires Above.

I thank the mighty oaks
and return
to the Oconaluftee.

He speaks.
I listen.

"Remember who you are!"
he whispers into my troubled soul.
"No one and no thing can change this!"

I listen silently as he stutters swiftly
over the smooth and silky rocks,
blending his wisdom into my ideas.

A wash of waves from deep within
brings the spirit horses.
I ride away.

The river has spoken.
I have listened.
I have healed.

AT KITUWAH

Her dark head is bent low as she and the necklace she is creating are becoming one. So involved with her work, she is almost oblivious to the goings on around her. People have begun to file into the Asheville Civic Center now, wanting to get a view of American Indians. Not the "Hollywood" type they see on the movie screens and not the "Wannabes" that assemble every full moon for a sweat. These dancers, artists, and crafts people are real Indians. The kind they want their children to see—the kind to write back home about.

The belly of the civic center, swollen with colorful American Indian artwork, blankets, beads and crafts, looks as though it will burst into one brilliant stream of colored lights at any moment. The center's auditorium heart beats in slow, methodical, hypnotic thumps as dancers of many nations parade around in their brilliantly colored traditional regalia—the feathers in their black hair bouncing in unison with each meaningful step as they dance their cultures alive. The unique clinking sound of rolled-up snuff can lids tied to several of the women's dresses announces a modern day homage to their grandmothers' use of shell rattles filled with tiny pebbles.

The magical swirling of colors and the high-pitched voices of the accompanying drum group slowly rise to a crescendo bringing tears to the eyes of the most sensitive. Later, after these exhibitions of Traditional, Fancy, Grass, Jingle, and Shawl dances, Elders will share some of the wisdom they have been chosen to preserve with those who care to listen.

Soon people begin stopping in front of her table, admiring her work, asking prices, inquiring about specific pieces. Her Cherokee jewelry, along with tiny handwoven baskets, is laid out for display. A small sign over one delicate creation reads:

```
Corn Bead Bracelet
```

"What is this corn bread bracelet?" asks a woman draped in turquoise jewelry.

A wide smile, making an already beautiful face even more so, flashes before the answer. "No, it is not corn bread, it is corn bead." Leaning over the bracelet she continues her explanation. "These are perfect for making jewelry. I just push the pin through the centers and they string naturally."

"Well!" says the turquoise woman, suddenly turning to walk away.

Looking at the bracelet for a long moment, she wonders aloud to herself if maybe she should change the sign. There may be others who will also misread it. But the sign is correct: it reads true. How could she change the truth?

After selling a few pieces of her craft, she settles back down to continue working on the necklace, humming a little tune to herself.

This story is for Betty Maney of the Big Cove Community in Cherokee, North Carolina

INSIDE THE CIRCULAR WOMB

The cedar knots of trees rise up
nipples of breasts waiting to be caressed
by the hands of the stroking winds.

The waters of the soul roll
back and forth in foreplay
across the spine.

Paths of luscious lilacs trail themselves
between blue wild indigos of the moment
and anxious anemones of tomorrow.

The green meadows glow
with the white fires of invisible beings
searching for themselves in other forms.

Magical arrows shoot into waiting rainbows
which scatter and rain down
gold and silver stars

hitting inside the circular womb
making musical notes from which
memories grow strong and straight, leaving

traces of truth slipping
into the voidness of the beyond
like a silent drowning.

Peace touches itself.

SELU

Aware of what is happening to the children
Corn Woman walks the fields, carrying knowledge
from where the good medicine grows.

Pulling truths from stalks of corn
leaning into the winds, the teachings of long ago
become renewed with every grain the children swallow.

Keep in mind that you
are part of the whole, she reminds them.
The future is planted within you.

Give to yourselves lives to be proud of.
Treat yourselves and others
always with respect.

The rocks are listening. The trees are listening.
The eagles are listening. The rivers are listening.
And the children?

They are destined to hear
the sounds of the sacred grains of wisdom
growing inside their hearts.

ESSENCE OF POETRY

In the stillen teardrop of a baby's eye
the deep cut lines of a grandfather's face
the swaying dark hair of an Indian woman walking and
the stalwart determination of a young ball player
poetry is at rest.

In the blank husky face of a tiny straw doll
the carefully chosen colors beaded into jewelry
the inherited designs in the woven cane baskets and
the hand-carved horns of the wooden medicine mask
poetry is at rest.

In the naked limbs of a stark spirit tree
the mysterious howls of the rising wind
the mirrored images cast on moving waters and
the delicate cloud shadows dancing on mountains
poetry is at rest.

In the nubbed green grass left by feeding deer
the intricate webbed homes of a water spider
the soft white plumage of a long-billed crane and
the eerie wailing calls of the lone grey wolf
poetry is at rest.

In the solemn reverence of ceremonial rites
in prayer-filled smoke spiraling upward
in circular steps of traditional dances and

in the musical tones of an indigenous language
poetry is at rest.

In the sudden quietness of a deep premonition and
the ardent purpose of an ancestral calling
poetry is resting, waiting, connecting, speaking
to all who are guided to listen.

INVISIBLE TONGUES

If you desire to communicate
with the *Nuhnehi*
go and touch the branches of willows
swaying in whispering winds.

Go and sit on sanctioned rocks
boldly stationed along talking rivers.
Go and sleep on breathing mountains
looking over murmuring valleys.

The Spirits are there
ever listening, ever hearing
and ever speaking
to you.

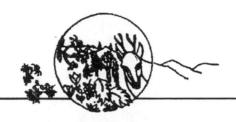

THE IMPORTANCE OF RESPECT

The Hunter

The hunter sits on a rock near the Hiwassee River, waiting. The man of medicine, whom he trusts to bring relief to his tired, swollen, aching body, has traveled up into the smoking mountains to find the plant that will give his rheumatic body relief. The hunter waits for the medicine with the patience of a rattler awaiting the warmth of spring. He knows the pain in his body is the result of his forgetfulness to honor the spirit of the four-footed one he killed to provide meat for his family. Accepting his penance with dignity for many days and nights, he now awaits the relieving medicine. As the red light of the dawn begins to illuminate his prayers, he steps into the quick running waters to soothe his body.

The Gathering of Medicine

Searching on the eastern side of the mountain, the man of medicine does not take the first, second, nor third plant he finds. It is the fourth that will supply the needed medicine for the man he has agreed to help. After a solemn prayer addressed to *Ada'wehi'* in which he humbly asks to take only a small piece of the ginseng's flesh to help the suffering hunter, he proceeds the digging of the fourth plant. Then, as in the middle of the night when a good dream is quickly snatched away by a sudden noise, he pulls the ginseng from its home in the earth. In exchange, he leaves a small bead in the hole where the plant was growing. It is right to honor the spirits of the plants with gifts in exchange for the help they continue to provide his people.

❦ ❦ ❦

In The Beginning

Little Deer runs swiftly to the site of the killing of one of his deer tribe. Leaning over the stains of blood lying on the wet grass of the forest floor, he asks the spirit of the deer if it has heard the hunter's prayer asking for pardon before the death. When the spirit tells him no, he follows the drops of blood to the hunter's cabin, enters without human eyes being able to detect him, and strikes this hunter with rheumatism.

The hunter's adversity is caused by his own neglect to respect a resolution made by Chief Little Deer long ago. At one time humans and animals conversed with one another and lived together in peace and harmony. But when the humans began to multiply so rapidly that they not only crowded their four-footed friends into the forest, but they also began to kill too many for their skins and flesh, Little Deer declared that unless a hunter asks for pardon before the killing of one of his tribe, this hunter would be stricken as a cripple.

❦ ❦ ❦

Compassion

The plants, who have always been friendly to humans, heard what the deer, as well as the other animals, had declared on their friends. Thus, the spirit of each tree, shrub, grass, and herb, agreeing to furnish a remedy for the diseases inflicted upon humans by the animals, gave birth to medicine. Unto this day, just as the man of medicine asks the ginseng to help one of his tribe who has been stricken with rheumatism, humans continue to ask the spirits of plants to provide the proper remedies for their ailments.

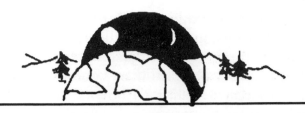

DREAMSTATE

At times
when I am sleeping
I follow the spirits of my grandmothers
as they drift along the heart–shaped ridges
of midnight–blue mountains
offering their myriad thoughts
of days long gone.

How strange it must have been
to see eyes the color of early morning skies,
skin the color of foamy floating clouds,
for the first time.

How disheartening to hear the words
"Your future does not belong to you!
"Your beliefs are invalid!"
And more painful still
to hear the command
"You must leave the graves of
your people behind!"

Motioning for me to follow,
the spirits of my grandmothers float through time
in their shawls woven with threads
from secrets of old.

Giving thanks to each new moon
singing songs to each day dawning
and bathing in the waters of sacred rivers
I watch as they perform these ceremonious rites
teaching me reverence for all things and making clear
the motive for every action should always be
for the good of the whole.

They speak into my heart and remind me
a dream can tattoo your soul:
Forever be respectful of where and with whom
you travel during dreamstate.

As the sun drags his giant red body
from behind the darkened mountains
and peaks into the mirror of his dawning
my grandmothers return to wherever Spirits go
and I awake into sleepy wonderment
of how we, The Principal People,
continue to survive.

RAVELINGS

Mother gave to the Mexican couple selling blankets
what she did not easily give:
Attention and a smile.

How did they find us Indians
way back here in this cotton field?
I wondered with my young girl's mind.

I suspected she knew them from somewhere.
This was before I came
to believe in spiritual connections.

Mother's eyes were deep and glistening
fresh and full of wonder and amazement of what the
world might hold for a
beautiful Indian woman.

I watched and learned my lessons well.
But I've not smiled at a Mexican couple selling blankets.
Not yet.

THE OWLS

Night time arrives.

Echoes of moanings
fly from the wombs of the mountains
as the feathered ones slip into
the unconsciousness of becoming balanced.

Where the sun goes when it dies
is inside the blue-ridged hearts of these mountains.
Into the abysmal achings of those
who used to inhabit this land.

Perched on their suspicion
the owls continue to watch the darkness
for explanations why The Cherokee People
were driven from their homelands.

At times
in the middle of passing reflections they are spoken to.
The Little People seek to tell their secrets of
what really came

down
from
the mountains
when all the Cherokee People were among them.

The Ustutli once lived here.
Remnants of its power draw these little ones into the
consciousness of now,
goading them to tell the truth to the feathered ones
who question.

This great serpent was a mystery to everyone,
including itself. Into the shading of night,
chilling shadows of its power float among
the blooming of the moon flowers

melt into the soft wetness
of the small lakes and running waters
circle the perfect eyes of the owls
and cause eruption of the secrets of The Little People.

Memories of this mystical serpent
come to the owls
in waves of persistence
now that they know the truth.

The Little People capture what is left
of the feathered ones' imagination
molding it magically into
the secrets of old.

They must now
trust the maker of their rain
that what has happened to The Cherokee People
will not happen to them.

The owls, nodding in sleepy agreement,
turn their heads toward the mountains at midnight
suspecting with their silent prayers that one day
respect will be given back to the Cherokees

who revere their homeland
the fierce Ustu'tli
the Little People
and the wise feathered ones.

E LO HI NO

Star Woman
will you continue to shine if all skies become choked?

Chanting Woman
will you care to sing if all birds lose their homes?

Working Woman
will you plant your seeds if all lands are exhausted?

Wandering Woman
will you stop to drink if all waters fill with disease?

Painting Woman
will you find true colors if all flowers turn to memories?

Medicine Woman
will you give consolation if all souls are angry?

Warrior Woman
will you protect your domain if all resources diminish?

Dreaming Woman
will you form the future if all nights become shattered?

Dancing Woman
will you keep in step if your heart grows heavier?

Dance on, Dancing Woman!
There are those who respect you
those who want to preserve you

those who want the children of their children
to inherit you!
Let go your heavy heart!

Shine, sing, plant, water, create, console, protect,
dream and dance!
Dance on, Dancing Woman, Dance on!

WATERLESS TEARS ON THE TRAIL

I stand here
with my dead child in my arms.
Soft I speak
so as not to disturb its sleeping soul.

Soft I speak
so as not to disturb all the spirits
who are now on their journeys
to the above world.

Otherwise I would scream
as the eagle screams to frighten its enemies.
Otherwise I would rake
hot ashes over my throat so as

to bring out the burning words
that I aim toward your hearts.
I am a gentle man with a generous mind
and a wounded heart.

The spirits of my people cry for
the lands that have been taken from them.
They cry for the difficult destinies
of those who follow

and they cry for the stones lying
inside your hearts.

TO CATCH A DREAM

She arises early again this morning to shake last night's dreams from her pillow. Every morning for the past month, she has shaken her floral–designed pillow case gently so as not to break any of her dreams as they float to the floor. She is looking for a special one—a beautiful, quiet dream embroidered in magnificent colors. One that will help her to escape the blandness of her everyday reality.

As she stares at her dreams lying every so softly on the bare bedroom floor, she notices one looks different from the others. Not only does it float several inches above the floor, it is brilliant and shining like her baby girl's eyes at Christmas time. Dare she pick it up? She has been fooled before—all that glitters is not gold— her grandmama has told her this so many times.

But this one seems bright and promising and she has nothing to lose. Scooping her dark hand under the dream and bringing it ever so closely to her ear, she listens. There is no sound but the frantic beating of her heart. She puts it to her lips, but there is no taste other than the perspiration above her upper lip. She puts it to her breast and her heart beat begins to slow. Yes, this could be the one she has been waiting for.

She pushes the bright dream inside her heart and waits. And waits and waits. Finally, it is time to wake her husband from his drunken sleep to see if he will go to work today. It is time to wake her three oldest children so that they may get ready to catch the bus for school. It is time to make it through another day—pretending, smiling, hiding the aching in her body. She is carrying her sixth child and she wants so much to find the bright beautiful dream.

As she brushes the tangles from her oldest daughter's thick hair, she thinks that maybe she should have tried to catch the dream as it floated from her pillow and not allowed it to drift towards the floor with the others. She will have to pay closer attention tomorrow. But for now, she will walk though this day as if in a trance. She will function properly—cooking and cleaning, watching a soap opera on TV, stopping fights among her children, and watching her husband drowning his self respect in beer and whiskey. Her mama's voice inside her head that constantly reminds her she should have stayed on the reservation and married her own kind, she will ignore. Just as she will ignore her daddy's voice that tells her she is not teaching her children the traditional ways of their people.

And she will wait patiently until sleeping time arrives again, bringing with it the possibility of a shimmering, colorful, safe, and quiet dream.

1890

The kind of bonnet my Injun Grandmaw wears
ain't got no feathers in it
but she wears it proudly just the same.

She married a man come from somewhere
over the big pond
just 'cause he asked her to.

From that friendly agreement
come a whole bunch of half-breeds,
one of which is my Paw.

He married a woman with dark black eyes
'cause she had some Injun blood and
'cause he liked her, I reckon.

And from that communal agreement
come me and my brothers and sisters.
Nine of us in all.

Some are darker than others.
Some taller, some smarter.
All of us are good workers though.

Rumor has it one of us
can talk with the moon and the stars
iffen she's a mind to.

It ain't been easy growing up
part this and part that.
Never really knowing where you fit in.

Some people get funny notions
when they know ya got Injun blood.
But my Injun Grandmaw says power is in the blood.

Paw says I'm all Injun cause I think like one.
I don't know.
I just think, that's all.

I know one day I'm gonna travel.
I want to see more'n tops of old mountains.

Although I do love 'em so.

Maybe someday the stars and moon
will point me in the right direction.
Tell me just where I need to go.

But for today I'm just gonna sit here on this old rock,
listening to the creek water running,
all kicked back and staring at them funny old mountains.

PURPOSE

Why are our cheekbones so high, Mama?

When you cry to the Spirits
your tears will have shorter journeys,
my children.

Your tears will have shorter journeys.

THESE THINGS I KNOW

Inside a mother's womb, light is the same as darkness
darkness the same as clouds
clouds the same as mountains
mountains the same as rocks.

Inside a mother's womb rocks are the same as flowers
flowers the same as water
water the same as breathing
breathing the same as touch.

Inside a mother's womb love is the same as honor
honor the same as Tsalagi
Tsalagi the same as birds
birds the same as babies.

Inside a mother's womb babies are the same as old ones
old ones the same as wisdom
wisdom the same as remembering
remembering the same as listening.

I am an old woman
and these truths rise up from their resting places
in my heart to share with you.
These things I know for I remember.

ANOTHER WORLD

I think my grandpa died early this morning. I can't find him anywhere. He's not in any of the usual places —down by the creek, talking with the rocks, out in the barn, smoking his corn cob pipe, or under the old oak trees, taking a nap. I've been looking for him all morning and I think he must have died cause I can't find him anywhere and my mama won't let me go into his room.

My mama is acting kinda funny. She won't answer me when I ask her where he is. She just keeps crying and mumbling something about she wished she had paid closer attention. I don't know exactly what she is talking about but I suspect it has something to do with my grandpa.

Finally, just when I think I can't stand not knowing any longer, one of the neighbors from down the road comes with his team of horses pulling an old wagon and stops in front of our house. I realize it's true—my grandpa has died—as I watch the neighbor man take a rolled up quilt stuffed full of my grandpa's body and place it in the wagon.

"Where are you taking him?" I asked.

"Down to the funeral parlor in Murphy, son. Now, you be a good boy and go and tend to your mama. She's a hurting something fierce."

But I was surprised at all the tears my mama was letting fall. She and grandpa had been at odds for as long as I could remember. Ever since he had wanted to start teaching me all about my Indian background.

"It won't do nothing but hurt him, Papa. He don't need none of that nonsense in order to get along in this modern world."

"Nonsense? Why a soul's got a right to know where he comes from and about his people! Just 'cause he's half white don't mean that he's all white! He's got Cherokee blood in him same as you and you know it, Daughter! Are you telling me that you are ashamed of it?"

But my mama wouldn't answer him on this point. She would just turn and walk away like she always did when there was something she knew she couldn't win out on with grandpa. He was stubborn and she knew it. I liked that in him.

I was really little, I guess, when he began to tell me the stories. Like the one about how the Cherokee believed the world is this great big island in the middle of a huge body of water, hanging from the sky vault on four giant cords—one at the east, west, north and south. And about how at the end of time, these cords will break and the world will sink underwater. I liked to lay on my back and look up at the blue skies whenever grandpa would tell me this story, and imagine those four cords hanging just above my head.

Then, when I got a little older, he taught me how to hunt for food and how to always take the weakest 'cause they would more than likely die anyway. And to always ask the spirit of the game for its permission before killing it. All this made perfect sense to me.

And sometimes, he would tell me about his mama. Her name was Totsu'hwa which means Redbird in Cherokee. I wish I could have known her but she went back to spirit a long time before I was even born. He said she was a right handsome woman, with dark eyes and braids all the way down her back.

And he said her mama, who was his grandmama, was quite respected back in the old days when all the Cherokee still lived in their homeland.

His grandmama knew more about herbs and trees and plants than anyone, and people were always asking her to help cure them of something. She knew all the ceremonies for gathering plants and making medicines, and practiced them most religiously. I forget what her name was, but I'm sure it was something pretty. He said he would see both of them again someday in another world, and that I was not to worry when he left 'cause he would always look after me and my mama, even when he went to be with the others.

Anyways, like I said, my grandpa died today and I sure am gonna miss him. He was kinda more like my daddy than my grandpa, and I sure am gonna miss him.

And when they put him in the ground, I'm gonna make sure that he has plenty of tobacco and his corn cob pipe with him, just in case he decides to stop and have a smoke on his journey to that other world, even if my mama don't like the idea. But right now, something in my heart tells me she won't mind.

CHEROKEE DAWN

We are as scattered smoke
the shadows of a willow.

The quietness of a rock
the waves inside a billow.

The guard of a silence
in which words remain asleep.

The summit of a mountain
of which there is no peak.

The nudgings of the moon
which lure the tides awake.

The secret of a volcano
which makes its passion quake.

The aura of hidden instruments
from which continuous music plays.

The moments inside the hours
which fill gentle days.

The flames of the fires
which burn yet remain unsatisfied.

The colors of the rainbows
which dance to become untied.

And we wait

as the Cherokee Dawn
awaits the day of her people's return

in quiet anticipation
of so strong a light it burns.

CONNECTIONS

We must go out and listen to the winds
even though they will never
reveal all of their secrets
we must go out and listen to the winds.
They will rejuvenate our souls

and the sounds they make
flowing and floating through the trees
are always the same
in any country, in any language.

We must ...

INDIAN WOMEN AREN'T SUPPOSED TO CRY

A troubled woman sits underneath a tall pine
watching the water from her tears
slowly dropping onto the velvet grass.

Two not of her race walk by. Why! She looks Indian!
I have heard Indian women aren't supposed to cry
they are so strong!

The troubled woman turns her glistening eyes
to them and speaks, a melodic accent cushioning
her soft words as they fall from her mouth.

When I was a young girl once in every while
I would go for a walk into these woods. On one
such walk I made a secret wish and left it here.

When I became a young woman I walked again
into these woods. This secret wish followed me home
and sat outside my window

smiling at me until I opened the door. Today
this wish disappeared. I have returned to the place
of its birth but it is not to be found.

The color of one's skin cannot determine
how fragile is
a heart.

POSSIBILITY?

There's not much left to tell
now that the Elders have all passed to spirit.
They held the answers to the questions
we seldom bothered to ask.

Like why the sun travels across the sky
during the day and the moon at night.
Which herbs to gather for which ailment and
how to be grateful for what we are given.

It seems we just pretended to listen
whenever they tried to share their wisdom.
What did we know? We were young
and just wanting to have good times.

But good times haven't lasted.
And now that we've all grown older
we wonder what answers to give our children
if ever we are asked

Why does the sun travel across the sky
during the day and the moon at night?
Which herbs should we gather for broken hearts and
For what are we to be grateful?

SPIRIT OF TRUTH

Into the clearing of a forest as dark and deep as a hurting heart, walked a young woman guided by the spirit of truth.

"Why have you come here?" asked a fat old owl. "Who are you to disturb my sleep?"

"I am *A ga li ha* of the Principal People. I have come to claim back the souls of my people from those who have kept them prisoners for so long."

"And who are those who have kept them prisoners?" the fat old owl asked with mild amusement.

"The spirits of doubt, frustration, and concern. These are those who have confined the souls of my people and made them afraid to return to their true selves. It is a long time now since one of my race has come into this clearing. By claiming my heritage, I am walking into the world of spirits."

"Indeed you are," the fat old owl looked at her with narrowing eyes.

"And you are the spirit of doubt!" she exclaimed.

"And why do you think this?"

"You sleep during the time all others are about the business of life, and you are awake when all others are resting."

The fat old owl chuckled. "Not all others, my child, not all others." He then leaned over and looked at her thoughtfully. "Nevertheless, you are correct in your assumption. I am the spirit of doubt and because you have spoken this truth into being, I will let go the hold I have on the souls of your people. No more will they doubt the worth of their race." As he spoke these words, he flew into the darkest part of the night.

"Thank you," said *A ga li ha* to the spirit of truth that was guiding her, and walked even deeper into the forest. For days she walked, never growing too thirsty or too tired, for all she needed to complete her journey was provided as needed, and only when needed. Her legs were like stalks of corn, strong and full of purpose. Eventually, she walked to a great old bear sitting beneath a dying oak tree.

"Who comes near me?" grunted the great old bear.

"I am *A ga li ha* of the Principal People, and I come to claim the souls of my people from the spirits of frustration and concern."

"There is nothing wrong with a soul being frustrated and concerned. It is the way of trust," yawned and stretched the great old bear.

"You speak wrongly. This I know for I have seen you in a dream. You are the spirit of frustration, for all you care to do is sit and wait. You have come to the middle of your path of trying and now you are content to sit and wait."

"But for what, *A ga li ha* of the Principal People, am I waiting?"

"Something more to frustrate you, I should think, so that you may continue to be frustrated with yourself and your path!"

The great old bear hung his head in the mist of her truth. "You are correct, *A ga li ha* of the Principal People. I have been sitting here for a long time now, sleeping mostly, and feeling sorry that I do not have the ability to accomplish my goal of climbing this oak tree. Now it is dying from the tears of frustration I have shed on it these many days and nights."

But *A ga li ha* was not moved by his story of woe and pity. "You have taken the joy of trying from the souls of my people and now I demand that you give it back! They are weary of their responsibility for their heritage and gifts to the world because others ignore or judge them! They need their souls to give them strength and endurance. Clear their souls of this frustration, I tell you!"

The great old bear, too frustrated to argue, shook his head in agreement, then slowly sank into the dark earth as the oak tree began to sprout new green leaves.

Satisfied, *A ga li ha* walked on even deeper into the forest, sprinkling tobacco along the path to thank the spirit of truth that was guiding her. After four days of walking toward the morning sun, she came near a cave cut into the side of a black mountain. It was here she heard the horrible loud laughing and cackling of a crafty old witch.

"Why do you laugh so? Why are you so full of merriment?" *A ga li ha* spoke without hesitation.

The crafty old witch turned to see who had spoken to her in such manner.

"So!" the old witch cackled loudly, arching her back as the young woman walked into the cave. "You have finally arrived!"

"Yes. It is I, *A ga li ha* of the Principal People. And I know that you are the one who has soaked the souls of my people with concern so that they are not grateful for their blessings. You are the one I have come to reckon with!"

"A puny little woman like you?" the crafty old witch screamed at *A ga li ha*, but the threat in her voice did not cloak the worry in her tiny eyes.

"I shall not leave until you agree to release the souls of my people from concern."

"And your people are too full of concern?"

"Yes. They cannot understand that to be grateful is to be satisfied and free from concern."

"And what makes you, puny woman, think you could possibly understand?"

"I know for I have been taught by the spirit of truth to look for the good in everything that comes my way, and to leave concern for the morrow to the morrow."

"Everything that comes your way?"

"Everything!" *A ga li ha* noticed the witch was beginning to shrink.

"Enough talk. Let go of the souls of my people!"

The disappearing crafty old witch spoke deep into *A ga li ha*'s sparkling black eyes. "I will release the souls of your people from so much concern, but it will be their responsibility to be grateful."

"The spirit of truth will forever remind them."

"And how?" the last part of the shrinking crafty old witch wanted to know.

"By guiding the spirit of gratitude to whisper into the ear of each new born babe and its mother."

A ga li ha then left the forest that was dark and deep as a hurting heart, and joyfully returned home to witness the many changes that were coming to her people. Their souls were cleansed of the spirits of doubt, frustration, and concern, and all began to share the joys and responsibilities of being The Principal People, as they had so long ago.

DREAMING EAGLES

Smoke–covered mountains are in my dreams
their strong ancient energy

calling
me into a period of creating
and intermittent resting

there, where there are no first people
we have always been there

testing
the realm of the spirits
answering the heedings of the wild energy

which blows its winds through the tunnels
of the minds of the mountains

seeking
searching for itself
in its own forgotten visions

shattering the thoughts of today
into the moments of the yesteryears

whispering
to the Cherokee what they know
to be the truth concerning their heritage

but never allowing too many words to
burn open the wounds of those

searching
among the melodies
of the songs and stories left behind

and my dreams
become white eagles

floating
ovr' smoky summits and
deep painful cuts into the sides of the mountains

soaring into a world which speaks promises of new
destinies because the old
ones have become abused

knowing
all the while
destinies are not to be altered

so the writings
and the songs and the stories continue

floating
in on the melodies
released from their storings of long ago

as the dreaming eagles fly
into the whiteness of themselves

watching
braceleted ladies disguised in the colors of spirits
slipping out of the caves

warning me to look directly into the eyes
of the ever-blooming, ever-dying world

sliding
down into valleys of forgetfulness
the secrets melt into themselves

only to be lifted up once again
on the wings of the dreaming white eagles.

GIFTS

Some secrets of old
are now being told
no longer hiding in the wind.

Speaking out strong
through art, poetry, and song
providing guidance now and again.

RUMORS

It was rumored that Addy May Birdsong would sneak into your house, touch your forehead with her fingers while you were sleeping, and change the course of your dreams. I had heard this rumor for the first time when I was about thirteen. Lydia Rattler, who sat next to me in Home Room, told me this because she had heard that Addy May was related to me.

"So what?" I had said back to her. "Everybody's related to everybody on this reservation." I had never liked Lydia much because she had ugly teeth that stuck way out and because she wanted to gossip all the time like an old woman. But she sat next to me that whole school year and I learned to endure her gossip, if not her buck teeth.

When I had asked my mama about the rumor, she said that lots of things were said about Addy May because she was different than most.

"What do you mean, different?" I asked in total sincerity. It seemed to me that almost every adult I knew back then had some sort of strangeness about them - mostly caused from alcohol, or from running out of it.

"Well," my mama had said thoughtfully as she scratched her chin the way she often did when she was trying to explain something in terms that she thought I might understand, "Cousin Addy May just has a way of stirring up people. She looks all the way into their souls with those black pitted eyes of hers and it makes people wonder if she knows what they've been up to." I had to agree with the part about the black pitted eyes. They reminded me of a tunnel that a train had just gone through.

"But you don't pay any mind to what you hear about her. She's your cousin and she's had a hard life, harder than most on this reservation, and so she deserves to be a little stranger than most if she wants."

I forgot about my "stranger than most" Cousin Addy May and all the rumors about her until one night it was so hot I was having trouble sleeping and decided to crawl out the bedroom window to get some fresh air. I was careful not to wake my younger twin sisters. 'Course I loved them with all my heart, but they could be quite bothersome when I wanted some time alone.

The night air was so cool and refreshing, I pulled my braids on top of my head and let it touch the back of my neck. It made me feel so good, I decided to take a walk down the road that led up the mountain to our house. The two other families that lived on the road were at least two miles away, so I felt like I had the road all to myself. I had walked for about ten minutes, staring up at the stars and the full moon, feeling proud that I was so brave to be out by myself that late at night when I saw Addy May standing there in the middle of the road with the moon shining down on her head like a flashlight. Her hair was long and loose, not braided as usual, and I remember thinking that it looked like a thick, black waterfall flowing down her skinny back. I was totally shocked to see someone standing there in the middle of the night and grateful that she hadn't heard me coming down the road.

She had her back to me, so I stepped into the darkness of the brush beside the road so I could watch her. She was wearing a long cotton skirt that was probably dark blue but looked purple in the moonlight, and a shawl of many colors was draped loosely around her thin shoulders. I watched quietly as she swayed her body back and forth, waving both hands above her head. The more I watched her, the faster my heart beat. And when she starting singing, I felt like it would bust right out of my chest. Her voice was beautiful, high pitched and full of rich guttural tones. Over and over she sang her song, swaying there in the moonlight. I could hear her words distinctly:

> First I was woman
> then I was mother
> Now I am woman again.

Mesmerized by her presence and her voice, I had no idea what her song was about, but I knew the words came from way down deep inside her. From the same place my moon time had begun flowing several months back when Mama had told me that I had become a woman. Addy May's words came from the connecting source to the earth that every woman has inside her, and my stomach burned way down deep in that spot as I listened.

I must have stood there in the brush for at least half an hour, watching her, listening to her singing, and feeling my heart trying to jump up into my throat. Then something happened that I never would have believed if someone else had told me about it. There were two female spirits come down from the sky and stood right next to Addy May's swaying body. One was real old and the other a young girl just a little older than me.

With quick, jerky movements, they began to dance around Addy May, looking kind of like the white curling smoke that dances around a red hot fire, and chanting in Cherokee. I couldn't understand all of what they were saying because I don't speak my native language proper, but I heard a few words I could recognize and realized the gist of their song had to do with sorrow and grief.

As I stood there, squinting my eyes, trying to figure out what was in the bundles each spirit woman carried in her arms, and to muster up enough courage to stay and see what would happen next, Addy May turned and looked directly at me. I swear she looked directly at me and smiled right into my eyes, never missing a beat to her swaying or a word to her song. When she did that, I ran back home as fast as I could and didn't tell a soul what I had seen that night. Not even my mama. As a matter of fact, I kind of forgot about the incident for a while because my thoughts were on other things. Mostly my new boyfriend, Roger. That is until I heard from Lydia Rattler that Addy May had been arrested for stealing a baby boy.

She had gone into John and Amanda Wolfe's house late one night and taken their baby right from his crib. The baby hadn't cried or made any noise or anything, so the parents didn't know he was missing until his mama woke up the next morning and went to check on him. He was only six months old but he was big for his age. I had seen him in front of the Spirit on the River with his mama the week before Addy May stole him. Amanda had gone in there to apply for a job and asked me and my cousin Lenny, who happened to be walking by at the time, to hold him for her while she went in the restaurant to get an application. It was really curious to me that I had actually held that same baby in my arms just a week before Addy May stole him.

She hadn't tried to hide him or anything, and that's why they found out so quick that she had him. She had just taken him home with her, and when Mavis Rose had passed by Addy May's house on her way to the Tribal Offices, as she did every weekday morning, she had seen Addy May sitting there on her front porch in an old rocking chair, holding him. Mavis said later that she thought it was kind of odd, Addy May sitting there on her front porch with a baby and all, but didn't know how odd until she arrived at work and was told that the Wolfe baby was missing. Of course she told all of them at the Tribal Offices what she had seen and they called the Wolfes, who had Addy May arrested. The baby wasn't hurt or anything, so the Wolfes didn't press it. The authorities let Addy May go after a good talking to because they didn't know what else to do with her, I guess.

Mama said she probably needed some kind of professional help cause she had never got over the death of her two babies who had burned to death that past winter. One was a girl, about a year and a half old, and the other a boy, six months old. Her old mobile home had caught fire because of bad wiring or something, and she hadn't been able to save them.

I cried after my mama told me that story. I cried like I had never cried for anybody before because I felt close to Addy May somehow. So I went to visit her about a week after that. I just stopped by her house on my way home from school one day to tell her I was her cousin and just to see how she was doing. She didn't talk much, just nodded her head, and gave me some water from her well to drink. I can still taste that water now, all fresh and cool and sweet from that dipper gourd she used. I stayed for about an hour I guess, just sitting there on her front porch with her, not talking. And that was OK with me 'cause I felt like I just needed to be there for her. She never mentioned that night I had seen her in the road, swaying and singing, but I knew she knew. And I knew she knew that I cared about her.

I didn't go back to visit her again, but I did see her at different times, walking around, mumbling to herself. She got real crazy after the Wolfe baby incident and people just kind of left her alone and made up more rumors about her to entertain themselves. She wasn't a real threat to anybody, and the Crowe Sisters who lived down the road from her always made sure she had something to eat.

I guess I just grew up and forgot about her for several years. There were my two kids and a husband to worry over, and I hadn't thought about her for a while until Mama told me that Addy May had died. She had got the flu or pneumonia or something, and passed away in her sleep one night.

"She's probably better off," Mama had said. I quietly agreed cause deep inside I knew that Addy May was with those two spirits who understood the song she was singing that night there in the middle of the road. The night she was swaying and singing in the moonlight, and I stood in the darkness of the brush, quietly watching and listening.

POX

Morning
Raindrops seeking shelter in strong silent grounds.

Afternoon
Medicine songs humming for sick sleeping babies.

Evening
Snowy clouds whispering secrets to waiting trees.

Midnight
Soft prayers floating upward on sweet grey smoke.

Dawn
Grieving tears slipping down tired mothers' faces.

Morning
Raindrops seeking shelter in strong silent grounds.

Afternoon
Medicine songs humming for sick sleeping babies.

Evening
Snowy clouds whispering secrets to waiting trees.

Midnight
Soft prayers floating upward on sweet grey smoke.

Dawn
Grieving tears slipping down tired mothers' faces.

Morning
Raindrops seeking shelter ...

VISIONS

Spotted Owl fell asleep under a dancing star.
This was the night he learned to dream.
His soul became a strong white bird
his mind a snapping terrapin
his body as strong as a bear
his medicine important and peaceful

and during this sleep
he touched something inside himself
that fell from that dancing star
and was never to be the same again.

Great Great Grandson fell asleep under a drunken star.
This was the night he began to hurt.
His soul became clouded with confusion
his mind a tangled spider web
his body as weak as a fish
his medicine stunted and ignorant

and during this sleep
he touched something inside himself
that fell from that drunken star
and begin to feel nothing but shame.

Grandson later fell asleep under a shining star.
This was the night he began to heal.
His soul became clear and hopeful
his mind intent on becoming whole
his body alert and mending
his medicine strong and powerful

and during this sleep
he touched something inside himself
that fell from that dancing shining star
and was never to feel shame again.

SACRIFICES

I stared at the mountain until I began to see it breathe. Until it was no longer a single, solitary rock, but a living part of the whole. It became the arms of trees reaching to touch the sky, the breast of the river swelling outside of itself, the mirror of all things past and all things present. It became more than a mountain. It became everything.

A strong breeze lapped at my face. Hard rain spat in my eyes. I could hear the heart of the Mother hammering beneath my feet and feel the beatings all the way to my knees. I knew the sun had begun its daily bleeding into the valleys behind me, but I could not turn around. I stood there and stared straight ahead until there was nothing left to see. Until night swallowed all things past and all things present. Until it swallowed everything. But still I couldn't cry.

The pain was so deep I couldn't touch it to name it nor could I find it with my imagination. So deep I couldn't reach inside and pull it out or push inside to make it go deeper. It was real. So real I could feel it choking itself on my innards. And so I waited, there in the wet dark, until it had it's fill of me. Until everything inside of me began to move.

All my memories began to remember themselves and all my dreams began to redream themselves. My heart hurt. My head hurt. All of my body ached and my eyes burned. Not because of what they saw, but because of what they were to see. And still I couldn't cry.

I continued to pray into the night and all through the next day. And I knew I would have died there that second night had the vision not come. The dark solidness opened before me and I watched the workings of spirit manifesting before me, gifting me with the answer to what seemed like month-long prayers.

Sweat beaded on my forehead. I smelled my own fear, tasted it as the beads ran down onto my lips. What I saw frightened but did not surprise me.

Mighty mountains crumbled, strong rivers flowed backwards, and age old trees uprooted themselves. People of all colors ran, screamed, begged for mercy. But the Mother had had enough abuse, enough neglect. She was shedding herself of those who had no respect for her gifts, for her bounties. As an irritated dog shakes off fleas from its body, the Mother shook off the humans who irritated her.

And then the air was still. Black and solid. The night closed around me as quickly as it had opened. As I fell to my knees, I knew what I had seen was to happen if changes were not made. If hearts were not cleansed of hatred and judgement, if neglected respect was not remembered, if the old ways of honor were not restored, my vision would become a reality. The Mother could and would reject us. For she is wise and knows that we need her much more than she needs us.

The creeping dawn found my eyes full of water. As I lay face down, my tears melting into the vastness beneath my tired body, I could hear the all-knowing wind whispering over and over:

"What is not loved and respected will be taken away. What humans attempt to control, eventually controls them."

WAITING

A clock ticks inside my brain
like old memories or worn-out photographs.
A tattooed snake slithers across my belly
carrying answers in its mouth.

One olden memory slaps me across the face.
It is the hand of my people's trials.
This photograph has its edges torn
around the color of someone's dark eyes.

There's little mystery left when the echoes
of the wailings begin to disappear.
There's little sanity left if you keep looking under
lying scattered treaties to find it.

I sit waiting.

The falling trees outside my window are dying
from the want of new colors.
Broken candles that should have burned down long ago
drape themselves along the windowsill.

Occasionally the dream-memory
of a ceremonial eagle feather still manages
to scratch its tip across my soul
even though it's been a long, long time now.

Where can all the faith go when it realizes
there's not much hope left?
"For your own good" charity
can be so deceiving.

I sit waiting.

For a while.
For a familiar breaking sound.
For a moment of silence.
For a tortuous memory to present itself.

I am inside the woman I believe myself to be now
and I don't know how far down to go
to find the one who cared for the ability
to make something out of nothing.

I do wish people wouldn't pray for me
unless they know exactly what it is I need!
I can't help it because
I don't know how to trust!

I sit waiting.

Last night I dreamed Indian children.
The night before I caught a beautiful raven haired
baby girl as she let go of the rope she was swinging
on and floated ever so
gently into my arms.

Maybe they will come to some of their senses
and realize all that's been taken
is all there is to give now.
Maybe not.

Here's a photograph of your old Granny as a young girl.
See her braids? She's Indian, you know.
What do you think of that?
An Indian with the name Marion?

I sit waiting.

Olden memories
like flies swarming a hot baby's face in mid-July
hover in the room where I sit
causing me to wander.

But trails of blood and tears are not a good place
to travel to during memory time.
I wish I could know
what I am really waiting for.

I dreamed the blood in my veins was
greensplotched with tiny baby terrapins
snapping at the sounds my heart makes
as it beats in unison with the pains of forgetting.

I sit waiting.

Listen to me sometime and I'll tell you the real stories
about how all of this came to be.
I'll let you witness the answer-carrying snake
slithering across my belly.

I'll share some olden memories of your Indian ancestors
maybe show you some faded, worn-out photographs
and we'll drink soothing herbal teas and pretend
we understand why I came to be this way.

Then perhaps you won't mind the sounds
of the clock ticking inside my brain
the nasty terrapins snapping
the mesmerizing children laughing
or the soft baby girl falling ...

MISSHAPEN HEART

When the warrior awakened, his face was blistered—red and glowing—so he knew he had been closer to his dream of capturing the sun than ever before. But a part of his being was not participating in this dream and so he could never be satisfied.

When he stepped down to look across the valley beneath his home, all the warrior could see were miles of darkened rains. His people needed the heavy light of the sun to come and stay for a while - to bring them hope and strength. He believed the rains had washed away too much of their happiness. If only he could capture the sun for his people, he would be the greatest warrior of all. He would be thanked and revered.

"When will this stop? When will this madness stop?" He shouted to his echo. "This warped dream is tearing my soul to pieces as it tries to release itself every night. Why can this dream not form itself to the shape of my heart so that it may surface and become reality?"

But it was not the warrior's dream that was misshapen, instead it was his heart. For in his dream to reach the sun, he had neglected the part of himself that lay hidden in the dark nights. The rich, intuitive side that chose to listen to the wind, to run with the raindrops, to reflect the sparkle from the stars. If he would but permit both sides to work together—allow the deeper side to provide the total dream and the shining side to put the desire inside the dream to work, his misshapen heart would form itself to his beautiful dream and allow it to materialize into the world. Then he would know himself as a total human being and realize one need not be the greatest warrior of all time to be satisfied. Then he could teach his people to be grateful for the dark rains as well as the bright sunshine—that both are necessary for balance and true happiness.

PAINTED

(for Lance)

Young man
searching
for rhyme in the desert
for reason

looking
casting away forbidden stones
listening
pulling inside welcome sounds.

Young man
searching
disappointed
turns to leave.

There!
just under
the feathered cloud
running

comes
his
hooved
gift.

Stopping
standing eye-to-eye
they lock
intuitions

a snort from
crimson nostrils
signals connection
is made.

In this moment
in this sacred
sought-after moment
spirit touches soul

and the journey along
the Red Road
through healing mountains
begins...

FOR THOSE WHO FOLLOW

Elders can teach you much
gift them with
honor and recognition.

Claim your heritage
respect your people
but most importantly, love yourself.

You
as well as all others
have a right to happiness.

And
remember
spirituality is paying attention.

TRANSFORMATION

Old Indian Healer walks toward his destiny
tap shuffle shuffle tap shuffle shuffle
blue jean cuffs dust cane-dotted moccasin tracks
tap shuffle shuffle tap shuffle shuffle.

Time-worn eyes roam the path
deep-centered thoughts block the scenery.
Hurry now hurry, Old Man
hurry to your Creator.

Sky beckons you
claiming your knowledge.
Earth beckons you
claiming your bones.

Spirit beckons you
claiming your animal.
Spread your eagle arms and fly
fly to your destiny.

Tap shuffle shuffle tap shuffle shuffle
Whoosh!

THE WAY OF BALANCE

In the farthermost corner of the moon, sit the faces of the children who have gone before me. The ones who cried and grew weak and scared; those who died along this trail my people are being forced to take to a land not of our choosing. It is nighttime now, we have stopped to rest, and I am remembering.

They came to our homes with bayonets, sharp and shining like the teeth of a badger, telling us we had to go with them. Old and young peered out of frightened eyes as we were forced to leave with no belongings. Mamas screamed as babes were pulled from their arms and used as bait to make them leave their homes. Papas shook their heads as they were forced away from the land that holds the blood and ashes of our ancestors. Like feathers falling when two hawks collide, our measure of self worth sank down onto the sacred, rich ground as we watched our homes being burned—our way of life dissolving into the smoke.

For many days now, I have looked into the depths of these men who came to pull us from our work and play, trying to find a reason for their hateful demands and actions. I have seen only dark spirits walking in muddied waters.

These men will not allow the women to gather herbs for medicine to help those who are weak. My little sister is sick—there are small red splotches on her body and across her face. My mama is swollen with baby and she too has become ill. My papa has been pushed into another group and although I cannot see his eyes, I feel his breath. I sense his voice telling me to be strong and to look after my family.

The coldness encircles us as we crowd around the too small campfire this night, and I realize that we who were once playful children have suddenly become tired old ones as we trek across this seemingly endless trail leading to a land we know not.

"West." I hear someone whisper. My mind fills with fearful questions that silently crawl from my lips as the rattlesnake crawls from the rock. What is in this Darkening Land, the place where the sun goes every evening? Will our bodies be burned as were our cabins? Are we to die there? Will the Little People be there to play with us? To tease us? Will they be forced to leave also? Driven away, as we are, from our homeland? I cannot believe this is what the Great Spirit has planned for my people.

My little sister crawls into my lap and wants to know if the *Ukte'na* will come from beneath the waters of the great river we have heard we are to cross and eat us. It always lies in wait, and now that we are in such weakness because of the white ones, will it have its way with us? No, I tell her and brush the tears from her black eyes. I am older and must be strong for her. I must not let this fear which clutches my heart show through my face.

My sister cries and my mama cries, but I will not cry. I will not let these people think they have crushed my spirit. I will not let them take from me the pride of being Cherokee; they are not worthy of such satisfaction. One day they will suffer for what they do to my people. I know this without being told.

A man rides by on his horse, counting the heads of those in my group. Ignoring the pleas for blankets and wood for the fire, he chooses to look at the tops of our heads instead of our faces. Maybe his job is made easier if he considers us to be cattle and not human beings. These men I cannot understand. I can no longer look into the eyes of those who are causing my people such suffering.

Some of these men are at times nice—usually because they want favors from the women—but most are so hardened within themselves that they cannot realize the wrong they do. When will they know that they do to themselves what they do to my people? When they push my papa, they are pushing their papas.

When they scream at my sister, they are screaming at their sisters. I am at a loss as to what to think about such men who do not know the meaning of being a part of the whole.

The moon has now gone to sleep inside the clouds, and I can no longer see the faces of the children who have gone before me. The night is dark, the wind is cold. I hear my mama crying for my papa. I hear my sister crying for her dolly. I hear the others crying for their homes, and I hear the old ones crying from pain. I am not crying—these drops of water are caused by the strong winds touching my face with their icy fingers. I am not crying. I am strong.

So many times I have heard my papa speak of reckoning. I believe his words. There is no fairness and no justice in this removal. Force can be a mighty enemy if all of one's weapons have been taken away before the battle. It may be many days from this time, but I know they who are driving us from our homeland will suffer just as my people are suffering. It is the way of balance. It is the law of the Great Spirit. It is spoken by the wind.

The fire is gone now, the ashes smoking into the night. I lay next to my little sister on the frozen ground and look up into the solid darkness. I say good night to the faces of the children who have gone before me. I say good night to my crying and hurting people. I say good night to my homeland. I cannot say good–bye.

OLD INDIAN HEART

There's a sick old woman who lives deep inside 'a me
and visit she does—comes up often just to tell me
how it feels
to be staying way down there. I guess she just
gets tired of hiding and praying

praying and hiding so she keeps looking for the
answer to heal
her old Indian heart in the secret wrapped up in my
old guts
but it ain't there. Naw, it ain't there
it's someplace else.

May be drowning over there in that white foamy river
may be crawling around underneath that pinkish rock
I don't know where the answer she keeps
looking for could be

but it sure ain't inside 'a me. Probably she
thinks I know where it
is cause I don't cry so much anymore.
Least not like I used to. I watch her. She just keeps
getting' older and tireder

tireder and older. It'll do that to her, waiting for me to tear
open that secret but I ain't 'cause I can't.
Look here at my eyes. Not the wrinkles
on top of 'em and not

the night circling around underneath 'em. Look
into my eyes. See? I'm still just a young girl
and I ain't got no answer for no old woman
living way
down deep inside 'a me.

She makes me think sometimes though and you know
what I think? I think the greatest epidemic today
is the broken heart. And me tearing open
my secret just to give her some old words

ain't gonna help that much.
Words can only touch a part of it.
What moves and heals the entire heart
can't be described. It's
beyond words and I don't know exactly
where it's hiding.

May be drowning over there in that white foamy river
may be crawling around underneath that pinkish rock
I don't know, all I know is I just don't know
where the answer she keeps looking for could be
because it
sure ain't here inside 'a me.

BEAUTIFUL CHEROKEE WOMEN

I see them
the women
the beautiful Cherokee women
they are walking, kneeling, dancing

walking alongside rivers, touching the waters
kneeling beside sick babies, asking for blessings
dancing to their music, laughing with spirits.

The strong Cherokee women
are walking, kneeling, dancing
I think it must be long ago.

I see them
the women
the beautiful Cherokee women
they are honoring, giving, praying

honoring their heritage, choosing to stay Indian
giving thanks for their bounties, planting more seeds
praying for their Elders, gathering the teachings.

The proud Cherokee women
are honoring, giving, praying
I think it must be long ago
it is not long ago.

I see them
the women
the beautiful Cherokee women
they are turning, making, changing

turning craft work into money, buying school clothes
making their voices heard, attending tribal council
changing the thoughts of others, remaining determined.

The dedicated Cherokee women
are turning, making, changing
I think it must be long ago
it is not long ago
it is now.

I see them
the women
the beautiful Cherokee women
touching the waters
asking for blessings
laughing with spirits

they are strong, proud, dedicated
they are
the beautiful Cherokee women of today.

GLOSSARY

Ada'wehi': Powerful Magician. Cherokee Priests addressed ginseng as *Yunwi Usdi'ga Ada' wehi' yu*—"Little Man, Most Powerful Magician."

Ada'ya: Principal Wood.

A ga li ha: Sunshine.

Beloved Woman—Also Pretty Woman; War Woman: Women council members who had the power to make important decisions; e.g. deciding the fate of captives.

Big Cove: Township on the Eastern Cherokee Reservation, Cherokee, North Carolina. Other townships include: Birdtown, Yellowhill, Painttown, Snowbird, and Wolfetown.

Creator; God: See *Yihowa.*

Darkening Land: West; Twilight Land; Land of the Dead.

E lo hi no: Earth.

Great Spirit: The connecting spirit between all things.

Green Corn Dance: Ceremonial dance performed annually to signify rebirth, forgiveness and new beginnings.

Hiwassee: A river which begins in Towns County, of northern Georgia, and flows northwestward to join the Tennessee River. The correct Cherokee form, applied to two former settlements on the river, is *Ayuhwa'si,* meaning "a savannah."

Kituwah: An annual gathering held every September in Asheville, North Carolina to promote education concerning American Indians. High quality art work, crafts, jewelry, etc. from various nations are made available to the public. *Kitu'hwa* was the main ancient settlement and gathering place of the Cherokee located on the Tuckasegee River in North Carolina.

Little Men—*Anisga'ya Tsunsdi'ga***:** The two sons of Kanati, the Great Thunder Spirit who live in the sky vault. Also called the Thunder Boys.

Little People: *Yv wi tsu na s di ga*: Men and women of small stature who live in rock caves on the sides of mountains. They are full of magic and love music. Sometimes mischievous, but usually compassionate and helpful to the Cherokee, especially children.

Long Man—also Long Snake: Cherokee reverent term for a river. The head of the man or snake was in the mountains and the feet or tail reached down into the lowlands.

Medicine: Gift of power and knowledge for healing, given to each being by the Great Spirit, to aid in feeling connected and in harmony with all of creation.

Nuhnehi: Invisible Spirit People; Immortals.

Oconaluftee: Name of a river which flows through the Eastern Cherokee Reservation in Swain and Jackson Counties, North Carolina.

Pox—Small pox: This disease was brought by Europeans to the Cherokee who had no immunity and no valid treatment methods. An epidemic virtually wiped out over half the tribe in 1738-39. Another epidemic hit in 1783 and another in 1866; both taking heavy tolls on the lives of the people.

Principal People—*Ani'-Yun'wiya***:** The name the Cherokee People gave to themselves long before others begin to refer to them as Cherokee or *Tsalagi*. There are seven clans:

Wild Potato, Bird, Long Hair, Blue, Paint, Deer, and Wolf. Clan membership is inherited from one's mother and retained for life.

Selu: Cherokee word for corn. Also used to denote feminine spirit of corn: Corn Woman or Corn Mother. Cherokee myth explains that the corn plant sprung from the dead body or blood drops of the Corn Woman. She is the wife of Kanati, the Great Thunder Spirit.

Spirits: Benevolent entities.

Totsu'hwa: Redbird.

Termination: U.S. government policy in the 1950s which stated Indians should break their relationship with the federal government and remove themselves from reservations and go to American cities for jobs and education.

Thunder Being—*Kanati***:** The Great Thunder Spirit.

Trail—Trail Where They Cried or Trail of Tears: In 1838, over 16,000 of the Cherokee Nation were forced by the federal government to leave their homelands east of the Mississippi River and go to Indian Territory, now Oklahoma. A stirring reenactment—*"Unto These Hills"*—is presented annually June 14 through August 27th in Cherokee, North Carolina.

Tsalagi: Cherokee. Middle or Kituwah dialect.

Tsvsgina'i : The Ghost Country in the Land of the Dead in the West.

Ukte'na: A monstrous horned snake with a blazing diamond crest on its forehead; reported to hide in rivers.

Ustu'tli: Very dangerous giant serpent or foot snake which haunts certain mountains.

Wa'ya: Wolf.

Yihowa: The one supreme being which consists of a unity of three spiritual beings.

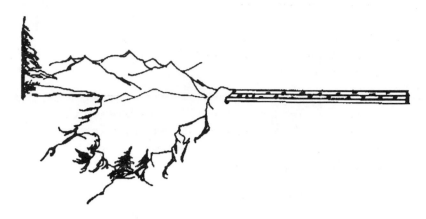

ABOUT THE AUTHOR

Cherokee author MariJo Moore resides in Asheville, North Carolina, where she is currently researching Cherokee Myths for a forthcoming series of childrens' books, gathering material for a non-fiction book on Cherokee women, and teaching workshops on American Indian Spirituality and Writing. Her co-authored novel *Beside A Singing Star-The Last Four Years With Willie Nelson, Jr.*, is expected to be published soon.